Lee

Faith and Reason

No. 22

Bampton Lectures in America
Delivered at Columbia University

Faith and Reason

Anthony Kenny

Columbia University Press
New York
1983

Library of Congress Cataloging in Publication Data

Kenny, Anthony John Patrick.
  Faith and reason.

  (Bampton lectures in America ; no. 22)
  "Lectures given at Columbia University in
April 1982"—Pref.
  Includes bibliographical references.
  1. Faith and reason—Addresses, essays, lectures.
I. Title. II. Series.
BT50.K43 1983   200'.1   82-22187
ISBN 0-231-05488-2

Columbia University Press
New York   Guildford, Surrey

Clothbound editions of Columbia University Press
books are Smyth-sewn and printed on permanent and
durable acid-free paper.

Contents

Preface

THIS BOOK contains the Bampton Lectures given at Columbia University in April 1982. I am very grateful to Columbia for honoring me with an invitation to deliver these lectures, and I greatly appreciate the many kindnesses I received on the occasion of their delivery. In particular I am indebted to President Sovern, Provost Swartz, and Professor Proudfoot for their courtesy and hospitality, and to Virginia Xanthos for her energetic and thoughtful assistance in many ways.

I first lectured on the topics of these lectures in a class given with Professor Alvin Plantinga at Oxford in 1976; I have since lectured on kindred matters at Cambridge and at Aberystwyth. I am grateful to the lecture audiences on these occasions for all that I have learned from them. I am particularly in the debt of Professor Plantinga and to Professor Elizabeth Anscombe of Cambridge for discussions on these issues stretching over years.

Faith and Reason

No. 22

Bampton Lectures in America
Delivered at Columbia University

1

The Virtue of Reason

THE TOPIC of these lectures is one of the most central issues in the philosophy of religion: the question whether belief in God, and faith in a divine word, is a reasonable or rational state of mind. In these lectures I shall offer an answer to the question: is faith rational? I shall do so by trying to define more precisely what faith is and what reason is.

Surprisingly, I have found it much more difficult to define what reason is than to define what faith is; and so I shall spend the first two lectures considering the nature of reason. Only in the last two will I consider the nature of belief in God, or faith. In the first lecture I will discuss the most popular philosophical account of reason or rationality, and I will reject it; in the second I will try to offer an improved account in its place. Then in the third lecture I will ask whether belief in the existence of God is compatible with rationality as I have defined it; and in the final lecture I will ask the same question about another kind of belief, faith in a divine revelation. My first topic is the nature of rationality: the virtue of reason. But I must first say just a few words about what I mean by "belief in God."

There are a number of different states of mind which may be described as "belief in God." We may distinguish between three senses of that expression.

1. Belief that there is a God, that God exists.
2. Belief in a doctrine on the word of God, as revealed by God.
3. Belief in God as trust in God and commitment to Him.

Belief in God in the first of these senses is belief in the truth of the proposition "God exists." It is a belief which might be reached in many different ways: one might believe it on the basis of a proof, or because one was taught to believe it in Sunday School or because a Godless world is too horrible to contemplate. It is a belief which may be held with varying degrees of conviction and which may find expression in many different types of behavior, from a mere inclination to answer "yes" to the opinion pollster's question "Do you believe that there is a God" to a life devoted to what one believes to be the divine service.

Belief in God in the second sense is more than the mere belief that God exists. It is belief in some different proposition on the basis that it has been revealed, or vouched for, by God. It is not so much believing in God, as believing God: taking something for true on the word of God. Thus, one may believe that Jesus

Christ will return and judge the world, believing that this is a truth which has been revealed by God, which God has given his word for. Again, one may believe that the children of Israel have a unique and permanent destiny, on the basis that this is a promise which God has made. Belief of this kind is not simply belief but faith, the faith for which Abraham was praised and for which Paul contended.

Belief in the third sense is more than the mere intellectual commitment to the truth of certain propositions as revealed by God. It involves a resolution to act upon these propositions: a commitment of oneself to the revealed purposes of God, a trust in His enabling one to enact them in one's life. It can be described not only as belief in God, but also as love of God: in its fullest manifestation, as the love of God above all things.

At the time of the Reformation much ink was spilt, and much blood was shed, about the relationship between belief in the second sense and belief in the third sense. For the Catholic tradition, faith consisted essentially in the intellectual assent to doctrines as revealed by God. Such faith was one of the three key "theological virtues" of faith, hope, and charity; it was a virtue, and therefore a valuable and praiseworthy thing, whether or not it was accompanied with the loving commitment to God, which was charity. If so accompanied, it was living faith; if not it was dead faith. For the Protestant Reformation the only faith worthy of the name, the faith eulogized in the Bible, was trust in and commitment to the saving purposes of God.

I shall not be concerned here with this question about the relationship between belief in the second sense and belief in the third sense. It is an important question, but it is a question of theology and of history; and in these lectures I shall be concerned rather with philosophy of religion, since I am a philosopher and not a theologian or a historian. As a philosopher, I shall be discussing the nature of belief in God considered in the first and second senses.

The question I shall consider is the most important question in the philosophy of religion. It is the question whether belief in God—considered in either of these two senses—is or is not rational, is or is not worthy of a reasonable human being. I shall thus be engaged in considering the relationship between Faith and Reason.

From the outset, however, it is important to guard against possible misunderstanding. Faith and Reason are sometimes presented as two contrasting sources of information about religious matters: thus a Catholic theologian might maintain that there are some truths about God (e.g., that he is omnipotent) which can be discovered by unaided reason, while there are others (e.g., that there are three persons in one God) which are unattainable without the grace of faith. I shall not be developing a contrast of this kind; rather, I shall be asking a question about both belief in the existence of an omnipotent God and about faith in the doctrine of the Trinity: namely, the question whether either belief is reasonable or irrational.

Reason, besides being contrasted with faith, is sometimes contrasted with understanding or intuition: some truths, we are told, are seen to be true as soon as they are understood; others are only discovered by more or less complicated, lengthy, and arduous processes of ratiocination. This contrast too, important though it is, is not of immediate relevance to the question I shall address of the reasonableness of belief in God. That question is concerned with reasonableness or rationality in a particular sense which I shall now attempt to make more precise.

It is important for human beings to strike the right balance in belief. One can err by believing too much or believing too little. The person who believes too much suffers from the vice of credulity or gullibility; the person who believes too little is guilty of excessive incredulity or skepticism. If you believe too much, your mind will be cluttered with many falsehoods; if you believe too little you will be deprived of much valuable information. There is no universally accepted name for the virtue which stands in the middle between the two vices of credulity and skepticism: a name which is sometimes used, and which is as good as any, is "rationality." It is in this sense that I am using the word *rational* when I inquire whether religious belief is rational. The rational human being is the person who possesses the virtue that is in contrast with each of the opposing vices of credulity and skepticism.

It was Aristotle who first made familiar the idea that moral virtues stand in a mean: that is to say, each virtue is flanked by two opposing vices, and each virtue is a disposition to have or do the right amount of something of which there can be vicious excess or defect. Thus the virtue of courage stands in the middle between cowardice and rashness: the courageous man has the right amount of fear, the coward too much and the rash person too little. Again, the liberal man spends the right amount of money on suitable objects: the miser spends too little, and the spendthrift too much. Adopting Aristotle's apparatus, I can describe rationality as a mean between skepticism and credulity, as the virtue which determines the mean in matters of belief.

Aristotle himself did not identify any virtue which had belief as its field of operation. Indeed, in the *Nicomachean Ethics* he says that intellectual virtues are not concerned with a mean as the moral virtues are. In the *Eudemean Ethics,* however, he says that the intellectual virtue of *phronesis* or wisdom is a mean between cunning and folly. A practical intellectual virtue, then, like wisdom, may be regarded as a mean; but when Aristotle comes to treat of mental states concerned with theory, in the book on intellectual virtue which is common to both his ethical treatises, he does not invoke the doctrine of the mean at all. This is because he concentrates his attention on those mental states which have only truths as their objects, such as knowledge and understanding. Because truth is the good of the intellect, and because whatever is known is true, there cannot be too much knowledge and therefore there is no need to try to identify a virtue whose role is to see that one has just the right amount of knowledge. But belief, or opinion, as Aristotle himself remarks, is a state of mind which may be either true or false. If something is false, then I do not know it, however much I may think I do; but a belief of mine may be false and yet remain a perfectly genuine belief. There is room, then, for a virtue which determines the mean, the right amount, of belief; and it is a gap in Aristotle's system that he does not consider this virtue.

What general account can we give of the virtue of rationality? According to Aristotle an act of any virtue must be in accordance with a "correct thought," an *orthos logos*. The *orthos logos* involves two things: a correct general appreciation of the nature of the virtue in question, and the application of this to the circumstances of the particular case. Only the wisdom of the individual, born of good will and experience, can determine the action to be done in the light of the circumstances; but the nature of the general criterion for a particular virtue is something about which there can be theoretical discussion, and about which philosophers may disagree, as they disagree, for instance, whether justice involves giving to each according to his deserts or to each according to his needs. So too with the virtue of rationality in belief: the individual's integrity, experience, and wisdom will determine what is to be believed and what is not to be believed in the individual instance; but general criteria for rationality in belief are something which the philosopher can and should try to formulate in the abstract. In so doing he will be, in Aristotelian terms, making explicit the general premise in the *orthos logos* of the virtue of rationality.

It is not a simple matter to specify the criterion of rationality of belief. It is easy to formulate criteria for the credulous person: e.g., "believe everything you are told." It is easy to formulate criteria for the skeptic: e.g., "believe only what you see with your own eyes." Anyone who followed either of these prescriptions would end up believing too much or too little. How do we formulate the criteria for the rational believer who stands between the vices of excess and defect?

It might be suggested that one should believe only what one knows. Perhaps, indeed, Aristotle's failure to introduce a virtue of belief beside the virtue of knowledge could be taken as a commendation of this criterion. But such a criterion would undoubtedly err on the side of skepticism, and would cut the believer off from many truths to which he has access even though he cannot achieve the certainty about them necessary for knowledge.

Shall we say, then, that the criterion of rationality in believing is that the believer should accept only true beliefs? Even this is excessively restrictive: there seems no doubt that in the appropriate circumstances it may be reasonable to believe a proposition that is, in fact, false. It is reasonable for laymen to believe in what they are told unanimously by the experts in a particular science; but from time to time the unanimous opinion of experts turns out to be wrong.

Many philosophers have proposed that the test of rationality in belief is that belief should be in proportion to evidence. Thus John Locke wrote that the mark of a rational person was "the not entertaining any proposition with greater assurance than the proofs it is built upon will warrant." In our own time W. V. O. Quine and J. S. Ullian in *The Web of Belief* have written: "Insofar as we are rational in our beliefs . . . the intensity of belief will tend to correspond to the firmness of the available evidence. Insofar as we are rational, we will drop a belief when we have tried in vain to find evidence for it." Similar quotations could be collected from many philosophers who came between Locke and Quine.

If this is the correct criterion of right belief, then it is clear what we must do in order to decide whether belief in God is rational. We have to discover whether the evidence for the existence of God is sufficient to warrant the degree of assent characteristic of a believer. In a later lecture, I shall consider the question whether there is evidence for the existence of God, and if so, what it may be. But in the present lecture I wish rather to question whether it is correct to say, as so many distinguished philosophers have said, that the mark of rationality is the proportioning of one's belief to the evidence. I want to ask whether a person can believe something rationally without having evidence for that belief. Can there be rational beliefs for which there is no evidence at all?

To answer this, we must inquire what kind of thing *evidence* is. A proposition may itself be evident, or it may be something for which other propositions provide evidence. Propositions which are themselves evident may either be self-evident (as that $2 + 2 = 4$) or be evident to the senses (as that it is snowing as I write this). Such evident propositions may provide evidence for propositions which are not in themselves evidence: as the occurrence of muddy marks on the carpet (evident to the senses) may provide evidence that the children have returned from school (not yet evident to sight or hearing); or as a long multiplication may prove, from self-evident truths like $2 \times 2 = 4$ and $3 \times 4 = 12$, such non-self-evident truths as $34 \times 13 = 442$.

Things which are evident may be said to be believed without evidence. Certainly there is no other proposition put forward as evidence for them. It is a mistake, I believe, to regard propositions which are evident to the senses as being known by inference from propositions about appearances: my knowledge that it is snowing is not a deduction from propositions about snowlike visual impressions. It is equally a mistake to regard self-evident propositions as resting on themselves as evidence: nothing can provide evidence for itself, any more than a witness can corroborate his own story. So evident propositions are believed without evidence.

It is clearly rational to believe what is self-evident, or evident to the senses. To this extent, therefore, it is rational sometimes to accept propositions without evidence. Those who say that rational belief must be proportioned to evidence must therefore to this extent modify their position. Most would be happy to accept the modification as compatible with what they really wished to maintain. A belief is rational if it is in a proposition which is self-evident, evident to the senses, or is in proportion to the evidence provided for it by such propositions. Rational belief, then, will either itself be evident, or be based directly or indirectly on what is evident.

Many philosophers, both theists and atheists, have accepted this criterion for the rationality of belief. Many theists have regarded it as appropriate to apply this test of rationality to belief in the existence of God. Naturally, being theists, they maintained that when the test was applied to the belief it passed the test. For Aquinas belief in God could be shown to be rational because the existence of God followed deductively from propositions which were evident to the senses, such as "some things move" and "some things, e.g., pepper and ginger, are hot." For Descartes the belief was rational because it was self-evident, or rather it could be made so by careful meditation on the concept of God, meditation articulated in the celebrated ontological argument for God's existence. Atheist philosophers, on the other hand, such as Bertrand Russell, have rejected the existence of God on the grounds that there was insufficient evidence for it. Common to theists like Aquinas and Descartes, and to an atheist like Russell, is the premise that the rationality of a belief must be tested by its relationship to a set of basic propositions which form the foundations of knowledge. This common belief has been given the apt name "foundationalism" by Professor Alvin Plantinga. I am greatly indebted to Plantinga's work, and I intend to develop my account of rationality in belief by expounding and criticizing the discussion of foundationalism in a number of recent papers of Plantinga, in particular his essay "Is Belief in God Rational?"[1]

Plantinga takes as a spokesman for foundationalism W. K. Clifford, the author of the famous essay "The Ethics of Belief."[2] Clifford sums up his view by saying "It is wrong always, everywhere, and for anyone to believe anything upon insufficient evidence." He makes clear that he believes that anyone who believes in the existence of God does so on insufficient evidence and therefore sins against the ethics of belief; is guilty, in our terms, of the vice of credulity.

The essence of the Cliffordian position, according to Plantinga, is that there is a set of propositions F such that my belief in God is rational if and only if it is evident with respect to F. Let us call the assemblage of beliefs a person holds, together with the various logical and epistemic relations that hold among them, that person's *noetic structure*. Then the set F will constitute the foundations of the noetic structure; and for each person S a proposition p will be rationally acceptable for S only if p is evident with respect to F.

Now is belief in God evident with respect to *F?* May not, Plantinga asks, belief in God itself be a member of *F*, and be itself part of the foundations of a rational noetic structure? No, says the classical foundationalist: the only propositions which properly belong in the foundations are those which are self-evident or evident to the senses. (According to some foundationalists, whom Plantinga discusses at length, even propositions which are evident to the senses, such as "it is snowing" do not properly belong in the foundations: their place should be taken by incorrigible propositions concerning immediate experience. But this is an unnecessary complication based on a misunderstanding of the nature of propositions which are manifest to the senses, and we need not pursue it.)

We must ask, what is self-evidence? Plantinga makes two points: self-evidence is relative to persons, so that what is self-evident to one person need not be self-evident to another; and self-evidence has two components, one epistemological and the other phenomenological. First, the epistemic component: a proposition is self-evident only if it is known immediately. Second, the phenomenological component: a self-evident proposition has about it "a kind of luminous aura or glow when you bring it to mind or consider it": what Descartes called "clarity" and Locke called an "evident luster."

The question arises: how does one know whether a thing is self-evident? For not everything that seems self-evident turns out to be so. It seems self evident, for instance, that some classes are members of themselves: the class of classes is itself a class. It seems self-evident that others are not: the class of men is not a man. It seems self-evident, further, that every class either is or is not a member of itself, so that there is a class of classes which are not members of themselves. But Russell has shown that this, so far from being self-evident, is not true and does not even make sense. The appearance of self-evidence, therefore, is no guarantee of self-evidence.

The foundationalist, therefore, if he is to justify his appeal to self-evidence, must accept some such proposition as "whatever seems self-evident is very likely true." But such a proposition is neither self-evident, nor evident to the senses: so its acceptance violates the foundationalist's canon of rationality, if he accepts it, as he does, without reason as basic. Moreover the foundationalist's canon itself, that nothing is to be accepted as basic unless it is self-evident, or manifest to the senses (or, in the other version of foundationalism, incorrigible), is itself something which he accepts as basic; so he is hoist with his own petard, for it is itself neither self-evident nor manifest to the senses nor incorrigible. Why should we accept such a canon?

> The answer [Plantinga concludes] is that there is no reason at all for accepting (it): it is no more than a bit of intellectual imperialism on the part of the foundationalist. He means to commit himself to reason and to nothing more; he therefore declares irrational any noetic structure that contains more—belief in God for

example—in its foundations. But here there is no reason for the theist to follow his example; the believer is
not obliged to take his word for it.

A mature theist commits himself to belief in God: this
means that he accepts belief in God as basic. There is
nothing, Plantinga affirms, contrary to reason or irrational in so doing. Let us consider how far Plantinga
has succeeded in establishing this point.

I agree with Plantinga that the phenomenological
feature which some philosophers have seen as a mark
of self-evidence is not a guarantee of truth: a proposition I entertain may possess an evident luster and be
false for all that. Again, however vehement an impulse
I may have to assent to a sentence I mentally rehearse,
the sentence may be false or even sheer nonsense.
There is no threshold of vividness or critical degree of
compulsiveness which ensures truth. We can record
this philosophical insight either by saying that self-
evidence is no guarantee of truth, or by saying that
not everything that appears self-evident is genuinely
self-evident. I share Plantinga's preference for the second alternative, reserving "self-evident" for propositions which are both vividly assent-compelling and
true. The evident luster is the appearance of self-evidence: only if it attaches to true propositions is it really
self-evident.

I agree also with Plantinga's principal point that
it may be rational to accept a proposition though it is
neither self-evident nor evident to the senses, nor held
on the basis of any reasons. There are many such

propositions that I hold myself: such as, that I am awake, that human beings sleep and die, that there is a continent called Australia where I have never been; that there have been Christians for about two thousand years. I claim that I am rational in accepting all these propositions, and in no way guilty of credulity.

My complaint to Plantinga is that one must go much further that he has done if one is to make any substantial contribution to answering the question "Is belief in God rational?" "So far" he says at the end of his paper "we have found no reason at all for excluding belief in God from the foundations. So far we have found no reason at all for believing that belief in God cannot be basic in a rational noetic structure." I agree that belief in God is not shown to be irrational merely because it is a belief which is not based on reasons while not having as its object a proposition which is self-evident or evident to the senses. But Plantinga has not shown us why what goes for belief in the proposition "there is a God" may not go for belief in any proposition whatever.[3] For all he has shown there would be nothing irrational in a noetic structure which included among its foundations "there is no God." W. K. Clifford could include among *his* foundations the proposition that a noetic structure including belief in God as basic is irrational; and he could do so with perfect propriety provided that he did not go on, as in fact he did, to subscribe to a theory which said that only self-evident and incorrigible propositions could properly be included in the foundations.

We may wonder whether there may not be criticisms of the rationality of people's beliefs based on grounds other than the complaint that their basic beliefs go beyond the austere limits of what is self-evident and manifest to the senses. If not, then it seems we must accept with a shrug that different people's noetic structures may differ in just the way that one man's meat is another man's poison. A's noetic foundations include "God exists," B's include "there is no God," C's include "I am Napoleon," and D's include a design for perpetual motion. Should we worry about this? Do we not glory in being a tolerant and pluralistic society?

It may be that the human condition is as bad as this: but surely we should try harder to see whether we can give a better account of rationality. Just because the criterion for correct belief given by the classical foundationalist fails, we should not conclude prematurely that no criterion can be given which will help to distinguish between rational and irrational beliefs, between sense and folly, between sanity and madness. In the next lecture I shall try to offer such a criterion; in the remainder of this I shall offer some prolegomena to guide us in the search.

Let us go back to the propositions which I claimed to believe rationally for no reason. You may have been surprised by some of the examples I gave. No doubt the propositions were not self-evident and did not report anything that was manifest to the senses: but surely I can give reasons for my beliefs that human beings die, that there is an Australia, that there have been Christians for roughly two millennia. And if I cannot offer reasons to convince you that I am awake, it is only because if you do not already believe that, you will not take anything coming out of my mouth as constituting the offering of reasons.

This last point brings out an important feature of the activity of giving reasons. If I am to give someone a reason for believing that p, it is not enough that I should point to a proposition q which he accepts and which entails p (as "I am giving you reasons" entails "I am awake"). Something further is necessary, which is difficult to give a precise philosophical account of, but which Aristotle summed up when he said that the premisses of an informative piece of reasoning had to be "better known than" the conclusion.

So too in my own case: p can only be the reason, or a reason, why I hold q if p is in a more basic position in my noetic structure than q. It is because of this that I maintain that there are no reasons on the basis of which I believe such propositions as that "there is an Australia."

If I were asked to think of reasons why I believe in Australia, no doubt there might come to mind such things as that I have often seen the continent marked on maps, I have friends who have lived there, I have had letters from there, seen planes depart thither, seen pictures of Australian cities and deserts, drunk Australian wine, seen Australian animals in zoos, and so on.

Two things are striking about this list. The first is that each item, taken in turn, provides on the whole rather slender evidence for the existence of Australia. All I saw, for instance, was the word "Australia" on the label of the wine bottle, or on the kangaroo's cage. However, it might be urged, taken collectively, these rather flimsy strands of evidence combine to provide substantial support for the proposition.

But the second, more important feature to notice is this. If any one of the "reasons" for believing in Australia turned out to be false, even if *all* the considerations I could mention proved illusory, much less of my noetic structure would collapse than if it turned out that Australia did not exist. I have only hazy and fragmentary memories of most of the things I might cite as reasons, and most of the things which have, over my life, led to my present firm conviction of the existence of Australia have long been forgotten. Even those which I remember clearly—like looking at an atlas last night—are far less fundamental to my noetic structure than the proposition that there is an Australia. If the atlas had not contained a map of Australia, I would have regarded this as a defect in the atlas, not as disconfirming my belief in the continent; conversely, if the atlas had shown a large continent in the Pacific Ocean at the latitude of California, I would not have taken this as evidence for the existence of such a continent, but rather as indicating that the atlas was not what it seemed. No doubt I cannot seriously contemplate the possibility that all the atlases I have seen have been spoofs cruelly placed in my way, or that I have quite misunderstood the nature of atlases. No doubt so much of my noetic structure would collapse if I came to suspect this that I cannot conceive of coming to regard all the evidence in atlases for the existence of Australia as dubious. But however that may be, the collapse would be minor compared with the havoc in my noetic structure if—*per impossibile* it turned out that Australia did not exist.

That is why I say that my belief in the existence of Australia is not based on reasons. There are no other beliefs which I have which could be used to support the claim that Australia exists which are better known to me, more firmly established in my noetic structure, than is that proposition itself. If there was any conflict between the types of information which I could give to support my belief in Australia—travelers' tales, or works of geographical reference or the like—it would be these latter, and not my belief in Australia which would have to give way. The proposition that there is an Australia sets the standard by which anything that might be offered as evidence on the topic would be judged credible or incredible. This shows that the proposition is not, in my noetic structure, related to such items in the way that conclusions are related to evidence.

I do not claim that no one's belief in the existence of Australia could be based on reasons, or that my own was never at any time of my life based on reasons. The belief in Australia in a young child today, or of an educated European adult in the eighteenth century, rests on reasons. The basic role of an item in a noetic structure is something which is relative to persons and to times. This is an important point to bear in mind in the context of belief in God. Suppose that Plantinga is justified in saying that for him belief in God is basic: that it is something which he quite properly believes without any reasons. Then his belief in God is not based on any reasons. But that would not prevent him from being able to give reasons to me why I should believe in God. For belief in God is not basic for me as belief in Australia is; and Plantinga might be able to show me that the existence of God was entailed by propositions which are basic for me—which are, perhaps, evident to the senses like "some things move" and the other premisses of Aquinas' five ways.

Though a belief may be basic for one person and not for another, there are some beliefs which must be basic for everyone. Among my basic beliefs is the belief that other human beings sleep. If this is false, then my whole noetic structure collapses; this is something I know if I know anything at all. This, which I can say of myself, all other sane human beings can say also of themselves. If a belief of this kind were to turn out mistaken, one's entire noetic structure, including the whole methodology of distinguishing true from false, would completely collapse. If any beliefs deserve to be called foundations of knowledge, these surely do.

Let me try to suppose that no one else has ever slept: that throughout my life anyone who has appeared to me to be sleeping has in fact been awake, and that everyone has been united against me in a gigantic and unanimous hoax. If I could seriously entertain that supposition, what reason would I have to trust anything I have ever been told by others, or to trust the ways I was taught to tell one thing from another, or the meanings I have been told of the words I use? To be sure, my identification of objects and my verbal usage appear to have been corroborated over the years by the constant agreement of others; but if they are all leagued against me with the degree of skill and resolution that this supposition implies, then this reinforcement too could perhaps be the result of malevolent and unremitting stage management. Of course this whole train of supposition is literally insane: anyone who pursued it seriously would be quite mad.

Because of this, my belief in a fundamental truth such as this is unshakable. There can never be any reason for disbelieving it, since any candidate for being such a reason would be something which called in question the possibility of there being any such thing as evidence at all. How am I supposed to acquire evidence for the universal hoax? Someone tells me "Whenever you have seen anyone asleep, you have been deceived: we have all been fooling you all along." Would that not be evidence that *he* was mad, if he seriously persisted in the suggestion? Suppose everyone tells me the same story. Well, if I begin to think that is what they are doing, I shall have to give up the idea that I understand what kind of thing human beings are or do or say.

Fundamental truths such as the propositions that ✓ human beings sleep and die form a class of propositions which it is clearly rational to believe without evidence, in addition to the classes admitted by classical foundationalism. Such truths are neither self-evident nor evident to the senses: yet they are not believed on the basis of evidence, nor is belief in them a mark of credulity. One cannot give evidence for them, either to oneself or to others: to point to individual slumbers and deaths can only illustrate, and cannot provide evidence for, the general truths. For anyone who is old enough to follow an inductive argument already knows that human beings sleep and die, and will use that knowledge as a standard for testing any individual's claim to be exempt from the need for sleep or the necessity of death. In the noetic structure of anyone who has reached the use of reason such truths have a role which is incompatible with their resting as conclusions on the basis of evidence which is better known.

We have identified, therefore, a further condition which must be added to the classical foundationalist's conditions for rationality if we are to hope to characterize that virtue. It is not, however, an addition which ، will enable us to say without further ado that belief in God is rational, because the proposition that God ex- · ists is not one which must be basic to the belief-structure of every rational human being. Even if it is something which *can* be properly held as basic, it is not, like the fundamental truths we have just been considering, something which *must* be so held. We must consider further the criteria for assessing the rationality of belief. In my next lecture I shall attempt to formulate a definition of the virtue of rationality: a definition which will not have the attractive simplicity of classical foundationalism but which will, hopefully, be free of the self-stultifying quality of that definition.

Like Plantinga, we have rejected the classical definition of rationality as the proportioning of one's belief to the evidence. We have, however, refused to give up at that point the search for the *orthos logos* of the virtue. We have agreed with Plantinga that it is not only self-evident or sensibly manifest propositions which can be properly believed without reasons; but we have not abandoned hope of finding a serviceable characterisation of the class of propositions which are thus properly basic. In the next lecture I hope to offer such a characterization, and thus to offer a definition of rationality which will provide a framework for the justification of belief.

2

The Justification of Beliefs

WE HAVE begun to consider the conditions in which it was rational to hold particular beliefs. We rejected the claim of classical foundationalism according to which the beliefs of a rational person should consist only of propositions which are evident to the senses, self-evident, or else derived from such propositions by a process of reasoning. Such a theory appears to be self-refuting, in that this criterion for rational belief seems to be itself neither self-evident nor evident to the senses, nor is it easy to see by what process of reasoning it could be derived from such premises. Moreover, it appeared possible to furnish incontrovertible examples of propositions which are rationally believed without evidence, while being neither self-evident nor evident to the senses. Some of these, such as the proposition that human beings sleep, are believed without evidence by everybody who believes them; the difficulty of providing evidence for them arises not from their obscurity but their obviousness; there is nothing more certain which could be offerred in support of them. Other propositions, which I instanced in my own case by the proposition that there is an Australia, may be believed by some people on the basis of evidence or testimony, but can rationally be believed by others without evidence, because of the fundamental role which they can play in an individual's noetic structure.

It is not enough merely to show that the foundationalist's canon of rationality is self-refuting, or to give examples of incontrovertibly rational beliefs which fail to satisfy his criterion. For this will not be of any assistance in assessing the rationality of beliefs whose status is a matter of controversy, such as belief in the existence of God. That there are some beliefs which are properly held without evidence does not show that the proposition that God exists can be rationally assented to without evidence. In today's lecture I will try to take a step toward assessing the rationality of belief in God by attempting to formulate a criterion for the rational acceptance of belief in general: in later lectures I will apply the criterion so formulated to the particular cases of belief in God and faith in divine revelation.

A criterion for rationality is most helpfully formulated in two stages. First of all, we need to construct a canon for the rational acceptance of a belief as basic, that is to say, for the belief in a proposition without evidence. Second, we need to articulate the ways in which nonbasic beliefs can be based on the evidence of the basic propositions, or otherwise derived from them. In the present lecture I will try to do these things in turn, though I will spend much the greater part of the time on doing the first.

First, then, the criterion for basic beliefs. I offer the following, starting from and expanding the inadequate criterion offered by the foundationalist. A belief is properly basic, I claim, if and only if it is

—Self-evident or fundamental
—Evident to the senses or to memory
—Defensible by argument, inquiry, or performance.

This is a complicated criterion: its value, if any, will obviously depend on how the individual clauses of the definition are spelled out in the sequel. It is a criterion which has none of the attractive simplicity of the foundationalist's canon of rationality. On the other hand it has one advantage over the foundationalist's canon: it is not obviously self-refuting as that one was. While this criterion is neither self-evident nor evident to the senses, it is not necessarily impossible to defend it by argument and inquiry. Indeed I hope to go on and show you that it is so defensible. But of course I do not hold it, nor will I invite you to accept it, as a basic belief: I endeavor to persuade you to accept it only after reflecting on the philosophical considerations I shall lay before you. While not self-refuting like strong foundationalism, my proposed criterion, on the other hand, is not as hospitable to lunacy as an open-door policy of laying down no general conditions or restrictions on what can count as basic.

1. Propositions Which Are Self-Evident or Fundamental

To the foundationalist's category of the self-evident our criterion adds the class of fundamental beliefs, the beliefs which are basic in the noetic structure of every rational human being. Beliefs of this kind were subjected to illuminating scrutiny in Wittgenstein's posthumous work *On Certainty*, the treatise on which he was working at the time of his death. Wittgenstein was concerned with a particular class of proposition. These were propositions which, while concerning material objects such as the moon, or human beings, were yet not empirical propositions in the sense of being believed on the evidence of sense-perception. They were propositions which were not self-evident in the way that the *a priori* propositions of logic and mathematics claim to be, and yet are not believed on the basis of other propositions because there are no other more evident propositions on which they could be based. As examples of such propositions Wittgenstein gives "The earth has existed for many years past" "cats do not grow on trees" "human beings have forebears." It was as an example of this kind of proposition that I offered earlier the proposition that human beings sleep.

I called these propositions "fundamental" because

they are universally held as basic: all those who hold
them do so not on the basis of other propositions. I
also said: "If any propositions deserve to be called the
foundations of knowledge, these do." But there is more
to being a foundation than merely being basic: a proposition is a foundation if it is not only unbased in itself but also serves as a basis for other propositions.
And it is not at all the case that all propositions which
are basic serve as a basis for others. The belief that
there is a fly walking up the window pane is basic for
me as I write this—it is manifest to my senses. But it
does not serve as a foundation for any significant part
of my noetic structure, and if it turned out false, little
damage would be done to the web of my beliefs.
Propositions which are universally basic are fundamental in a different way, in that they could not be
given up without causing havoc in our noetic structures; but there is something misleading in regarding
them as foundations of knowledge.

Wittgenstein wrote:

> I want to say: propositions of the form of empirical
> propositions, and not only propositions of logic, form
> the foundations of all operating with thoughts (with
> language) . . .

He at once went on to correct himself:

> In this remark the expression "propositions of the form
> of empirical propositions" is itself thoroughly bad; the
> propositions in question are statements about material

objects. And they do not serve as foundations in the same way as hypotheses which, if they turn out to be false, are replaced by others. (*On Certainty*, pp. 401–2)

A proposition such as "the earth has existed for many years" is not a foundation in the sense of being a truth from which other truths are deduced, as one might deduce consequences from a hypothesis or an axiom; rather, "in the entire system of our language-games it belongs to the foundations." The language-game is not a set of truths or an axiomatic system; it is the whole linguistic institution within which one distinguishes between truth and falsehood. My picture of the world, Wittgenstein says, is "the inherited background against which I distinguish true and false." If I regard some proposition as being at the rock bottom of my conviction, "one might almost say that these foundation walls are carried by the whole house" (*On Certainty*, pp. 94, 246–48). This means that the metaphor of foundations is not wholly apt. Just as the relation of premise to conclusion is inadequate to explain the kind of support that propositions in my noetic structure give to each other, so too is the relation of foundation to building. A building may collapse if the keystone is removed, not just if the foundations sag. The fundamental propositions in my noetic structure stand fast, as the keystone does, because they are held fast by the propositions which lie around them.

The metaphor of the foundations of knowledge has a great hold on the philosophical imagination. It was given that hold by Descartes: but Descartes has a different metaphor to describe the conduct of epistemology. He speaks of knowledge as a tree—a tree on which can grow wild and luxuriant branches of belief. Cartesian critical doubt can be regarded as a pruning operation on a noetic tree to turn it from a diseased tree into a healthy, fruit-bearing tree of knowledge. No doubt I can prune the higher more wayward branches by sitting on the lower branches; but I must be careful not to cut off the branch on which I am sitting. The fundamental beliefs which, in the other metaphor, are foundation stones, are, in this metaphor, beliefs which can be pruned only in this way: beliefs which can be called into question only by something which calls itself into question. Just so, I suggested earlier that any evidence purporting to show that human beings never slept would have to be something which called into question, *inter alia*, its own evidential value, by casting doubt on the efficacy of human testimony in general or, more likely, on my own state of sanity. The role of the fundamental beliefs is, I consider, better represented by the arboreal metaphor than by the architectural one.

Wittgenstein himself came to prefer a third metaphor: that of a riverbed. This was more appropriate, he thought, because it took account of the way the role of a proposition in a noetic structure may alter with time.

It might be imagined that some propositions, of the form of empirical propositions, were hardened and functioned as channels for such empirical propositions as were not hardened but fluid; and that this altered with time, in that fluid propositions hardened and hard ones became fluid. . . . The same propositions get treated at one time as something to test by experience and at another as a rule of testing. (*On Certainty*, pp. 96–98)

2. Propositions Evident to the Senses or to Memory

To the foundationalist's category of those propositions which are evident to the senses I add those which are evident to memory. I believe that I had a bath in my hotel room this morning; no one else saw me and I did my best to leave no evidence; but I believe firmly, and not on any evidence, that I had a bath. Also I believe that I lived in Rome from the age of eighteen to twenty-five because I remember doing so. This has no doubt left quite a lot of evidence in letters, passport stamps, photographs, other people's memories, and the like, but it is not on the basis of that evidence that I believe it; for me it is something basic.

Classical foundationalists are unlikely to have any objection to the addition of the deliverances of memory to the category of basic beliefs. Some foundationalists, such as Aquinas, actually believed that memory was a sense, an inner sense, so that they would no doubt regard the data of memory as included under the rubric of things manifest to the senses. It is, I believe, a mistake to regard the memory as a sense, as if it were something like a telescope through which one looks at the past. No doubt, however, it is correct to regard the visual, tactile, olfactory, auditory and gustatory memory as being a sensory capacity; and perhaps this is all Aquinas meant. The point is unimportant here, so long as it is recognized that the memory, as well as the five senses, is a source of properly basic propositions.

Some other foundationalists, in more recent times, have thought that truths about the past were inferred, or deduced from memory images or other mnemic data. They would thus not be basic beliefs, but belong in the class of beliefs justified by their relation to basic data. Again, I think this is mistaken; memory is not any kind of inference from something which is more immediately known. When I believe things that I remember I do not carry out any inference from something which is a quality of my present thoughts or images. To do so would be impossible: what feature of my present thoughts could even show that they were about the past, let alone that they were a true record of it? My belief in the past truths I remember is just as basic as my belief in what I now see. Of course I can be mistaken when I think I remember something; equally I can be mistaken when I think I see something. To be basic is not be incorrigible, and to believe something as basic is not to claim to be infallible. We can all make mistakes; but not every mistake is a mistake in deduction, as the classical foundationalist of this kind claims.

3. Propositions Defensible by Argument, Inquiry,
and Performance

This third class is the most significant addition I wish
to make to the foundationalist's categories of rationally
basic beliefs. It is, in its own right, the widest class of
such beliefs; and it is—or so I shall go on to claim—
the one which is most relevant to the consideration of
the rationality of theism.

We must first make a distinction between the reasons via which a belief is acquired, the reasons on
which it is held, and the reasons by which it may be
defended. These three sets of reasons may be quite
different, without any irrationality, incoherence, or
hypocrisy. I may have acquired the belief that X's
marriage is breaking up by listening to lunchtime gos-
sip; I may now hold that belief on the basis of a late
night heart-to-heart conversation with X's spouse; I
may defend the belief to incredulous friends of the once
happy couple by pointing to the list of divorce peti-
tions currently filed. In the case of many of our beliefs
we have very likely forgotten how we acquired them,
and on the basis of what reasons, if any, we came to
believe them. That does not mean that we do not hold
them now on the basis of reasons.

I believe that the American Revolution was, on
balance, a good thing. I cannot remember when I first
began to believe this, or indeed whether I have believed it ever since I first heard of the American Revolution. (I suspect not; I seem to remember my ele-

mentary school textbook taking a poor view of the Boston Tea Party.) *A fortiori* I cannot remember for what reasons I came to believe it; but there are lots of reasons why I now believe it. And these, unlike the "reasons" I mentioned in my last lecture for believing in Australia, are reasons for myself and not just reasons I could offer to other people, such as my children, to convince them of the merits of the American Revolution. If the reasons were called in question by a skilled advocate of colonial rule, I might be willing to change my mind on the topic. In the case of my belief in Australia, on the other hand, I no longer have reasons, though no doubt I acquired it on the basis of reasons. Nonetheless I can defend the belief to others by offering considerations which, while not providing reasons for me because they are not better known to me than the conclusion is, might reasonably provide reasons for other people whose noetic structure did not afford the existence of Australia such an assured place.

So a belief may be basic in the sense of not being held on the basis of reason, but yet defensible to others by the giving of reasons.

In my candidate criterion for rationality I have distinguished between three different ways in which a belief may be thus defensible. It may be defensible by argument, or it may be defensible by inquiry, or it may be defensible by performance.

It will be clear enough what is meant by saying that a belief may be defensible by argument. A can defend his belief in *p* to B if B questions it, by offering

B propositions *q.r.s.* which B accepts and which either entail or make probable the truth of *p*. But why do I distinguish between argument and inquiry? Pursuing a line of argument may be, perhaps, the pursuit of a form of inquiry. The reason for the distinction is this. If A's belief is challenged by B, A may already be in possession of sufficient information to be able to show B the truth of *p*; all A has to do is to produce the information from his own stock, and draw to B's attention that it provides convincing evidence for *p*. But it may be that A does not have this information at hand, and has to take steps to acquire or recover it. In this case his defense of his belief must involve inquiry as well as argument.

The former is likely to be the case where the belief is one held as basic because it is better known than any available supporting information. The latter is likely to be the case with the more trivial basic beliefs which we acquire every moment of our lives while quickly forgetting how we came by them. But basic beliefs of various levels of embedding may be defensible by argument and inquiry, and if so defensible are perfectly rational.

If a belief does not belong to the other two categories of properly basic belief then, I claim, it is not rational to hold it unless it can be defended in the appropriate way. But to whom is it to be defended, and how successful must the defense be? Must the believer be able to defend the belief to just everybody, and succeed in convincing each challenger of its truth?

That would be an excessively severe requirement for rationality. On the other hand, the mere fact that somebody can defend a belief does not make it rational for just anybody to hold it. If wise and well-informed A can defend the belief that *p,* that does not *eo ipso* make it rational for any stupid ignoramus B to subscribe to *p* even though he has never heard of A and has no idea how A would justify the belief.

For a belief to be properly basic for a believer B, B must himself be capable of defending it against those who are likely to challenge it. The believer's defense may take the form of referring the challenger to someone else who can conduct the argument or undertake the inquiry. But even in this case the believer must know who, or what kind of person, has the appropriate competence. Otherwise the relation between B's belief and the third-party argument and inquiry is too remote and coincidental to provide a rational defense of his own basic belief.

We may distinguish between primary and secondary inquiry. There is a difference between working out the square root of 3.4567 and looking it up in a table; there is a difference between looking out of the window to see whether it is snowing, and turning on the radio while lying in bed to find out whether it is snowing. Equally there is a difference between carrying out an autopsy oneself, and reading the pathologist's report; between doing experiments in physics, and reading an up-to-date textbook on the subject. The first line of inquiry is what I call primary inquiry; the second in each pair is what I call secondary inquiry: inquiry which is parasitic on other people's inquiries.

The argument or inquiry which defends a basic belief need not be so successful as to convince the challenger: he may be an unduly difficult person to convince, or perhaps the matter is one on which there is no knockdown argument. But the defense must, by argument or primary or secondary inquiry, produce evidence for the belief appropriate to the believer's degree of commitment. It is in this way, at last, that we make a link between rational belief and evidence, and do justice to the grain of truth in the foundationalist's claim that belief must be in proportion to evidence.

Besides argument and inquiry I have listed a third way in which a basic belief may be defensible: namely, by performance. There are certain fields where the judgment of a person with a special skill or special experience is rightly accepted as authoritative, even though the judgment is not, and perhaps cannot be, backed up with argument or inquiry. I am told that some people in various parts of the world have remarkable skill as water-diviners, or dowsers, though neither they nor anyone else can give an account which will stand up to scrutiny of the methods by which they claim to detect water underground. If such stories are true, then it is reasonable to believe in the presence of water on the say-so of a diviner. This belief is, of course, not basic; the bystander believes on the evidence of the diviner's past record. But the diviner's own belief is not based on an inductive argument of that kind, but is basic. It is none the less rational even though not defensible by argument or inquiry: it is defensible by performance.

Similarly, old Farmer Giles may be able to feel it in his bones whenever it is going to rain. Whether his feeling is a reasonable belief is to be judged not by whatever he may say by way of rationalizing it, but by his success in actually predicting the weather. A shrewd judge of character may be able to predict that so-and-so will go far, or such a one come to a bad end, without being able to say in support anything which really goes beyond "You mark my words!" If he really is a shrewd judge, the success of his predictions will justify his and our belief in what he says.

With these explanations, therefore, I offer as a criterion for the rationality of basic belief that it should be a belief which is either evident to the senses or to memory, is self-evident or fundamental, or is in neither of these categories but is defensible by argument, by primary or secondary inquiry, or by successful performance.

Having considered the criteria for properly admitting a belief to one's noetic structure as basic, we need to turn, rather more briefly, to the consideration of the nonbasic beliefs in a noetic structure. These are the beliefs which depend on, are based on, the basic beliefs. The criterion of rationality here must specify the relationship in which these nonbasic beliefs must stand to the basic beliefs.

There are two principal ways in which nonbasic beliefs are derived from basic ones: by inference and by testimony. In each case the basic beliefs provide evidence or support for the nonbasic beliefs. But within the broad categories of inference and testimony there are several different kinds of support provided by basic for nonbasic propositions.

When a nonbasic proposition is derived by inference from a basic one the argument may be of a deductive or inductive kind. That is to say, the nonbasic proposition may be derived as the conclusions of a deductive argument of which basic propositions form the premises; or the nonbasic propositions may be hypotheses which are confirmed or made probable by the truths recorded in basic propositions. Deductive and inductive inference furnish an enormous area for philosophical discussion: I shall, however, say no more about them, but will turn instead to the topic of testimony, which is a much less popular topic of philosophical inquiry.

Belief on testimony, like belief arrived at by inference, takes various forms. On the one hand, there is explicit belief in what we are told by others: someone tells me something, and I trust him and believe what he says because he says it. On the other hand, in addition to explicit testimony there is what we might call implicit testimony, in which others manifest their beliefs not by expressing them in words, but by what they do and what they leave undone. One can believe something upon implicit testimony, believing a proposition because others believe it, though they have never put it into words for one. Much of what we believe—all the things that are taken for granted in society or in our group—is believed on implicit testimony in this way.

Perhaps it is not easy to draw a line between what is believed on the basis of widespread implicit testimony and what is simply accepted as basic or fundamental. Wittgenstein has pointed out that many of our most fundamental beliefs about the nature of the universe were not learnt but were rather swallowed down with things which we did explicitly learn. But there is no doubt that testimony plays an important part in the build-up of our world of belief; a more important part than inference whether deductive or inductive.

Professor Anscombe has remarked how much of our world picture is given us by testimony.

> Nor is what testimony gives us entirely a detachable part like the thick fringe of fat on a chunk of steak. It is more like the flecks and streaks of fat that are often distributed throughout good meat; though there are lumps of fat as well.[4]

If we say, for instance, that we know there was an American edition of a book because we have seen it, think how much reliance on believing what we have been told lies behind recognizing a publisher's imprint for what it is. My knowledge that I am now in New York, even though I have seen quite a lot of it, is of course based on all kinds of testimony: on maps, notices, on what people have told me. Even those who have lived here all their lives know largely by testimony that this is New York: as they grew up from babyhood that was what they were told by others— the name of the place where they live and its location in the world's geography.

I believe that the conditions laid down here give an adequate account of the rationality of holding any particular belief. Given that someone holds a belief we can ask: Does he hold it as basic? If so, does it fit into one of the three categories of properly basic belief? If not, is it derived by argument or via testimony from some properly basic belief?

However, something else is needed to complete an account of the virtue of rationality. For the conditions considered have all been cognitive, and have not taken account of the volitional side of belief or the relation between belief and value. Moreover a test of the rationality of individual beliefs does not suffice as a test of the rationality of a complete noetic structure. Each one of a person's beliefs might pass the test of rationality as we have outlined it, and yet his system of beliefs as a whole be wildly irrational. These two points are connected together, as I shall explain.

Belief is a cognitive state of mind: it is not an affective state like an emotion or a desire. Nonetheless, it involves an attitude: an attitude towards further evidence on the topic in hand. This is true even more so of knowledge. If I claim to know something—in the strict sense of knowledge which has exercised philosophers through the centuries—I am claiming to be in a position to disregard evidence to the contrary. Of course I may have to consider evidence in favor of something I know to be false in order to help a deluded friend, or to get clear about a philosophical theory, or to avoid offending a benefactor; but I do not have to consider evidence in order to inform myself better on the topic in hand; I am entitled to epistemological disregard. (Of course I may be mistaken in thinking that I am in a position to disregard conflicting evidence; but if so, I am mistaken also in thinking that I know.)

Not all beliefs involve certainty of this kind. Knowledge is not just justified true belief, because a justification which might be adequate for the rational holding of a belief would not necessarily be adequate for the rational holding of something as certain. But any degree of belief involves a degree of commitment. The degree of commitment may vary: a strongly held belief goes with an attitude of disregard, though not complete disregard, of alleged evidence which conflicts with the belief; an opinion held on balance goes with a much more openminded attitude to the conflicting evidence. And when a belief is based on evidence, the degree of commitment should be, as traditionally claimed, in proportion to the evidence (though, as we shall see, that is not the only factor to be taken into account). Basic beliefs too may be held with vary-ing degrees of commitment, and here the measure of the appropriate degree of commitment is not the evi-dence but the degree of noetic embedding. So criteria of rationality must take into account not only the con-tent, and the basis, of a person's belief but also the degree of commitment.

The second point which our criterion has left un-touched is this. The question may arise whether it is rational to have a belief at all on a topic, or to lack a belief on it. It might be that each of a person's beliefs was rational in the sense of being properly basic, and yet his whole set of beliefs was not. This could be so if he had beliefs only on a set of trivial and unimpor-tant matters and lacked beliefs on all kinds of things on which it was important to have beliefs.

For despite what some philosophers have said, there can clearly be duties and obligations to have be-liefs on particular topics. This is clearest, of course, in the case of professional people who have a duty to be informed on matters concerned with their profession. But all human beings need information on thousands of things which are essential for the conduct of daily life, and for their cooperation with others and for deal-ing with emergencies. It might be said that it is wrong to describe this as an obligation to have beliefs: surely what you need to have is information, namely true be-lief, rather than just belief. Of course it is, in general, important for us that our beliefs should be true, and this is indeed the reason why rationality is important in belief, not that all rational beliefs are true but that rationality is due process in the pursuit of truth. But just as there are some cases where a decision has to be taken, and it is more important that a decision is taken than that a particular decision should be taken, similarly there are cases where it is more important that someone should have a belief than that it be true. When I sit on a chair I believe that the chair will hold me; that is to say, the thought that it will not does not cross my mind. Better that I should always have this belief—through on occasion it will let me down—than that on each occasion I should first check to make sure the belief is true. That way neurosis lies.

So if we are to assess a person's noetic structure we must not only inquire whether the beliefs he has pass a test of rationality, but whether he has beliefs on topics where it is important that he should have them. The topic of importance is important and difficult: and it is obviously relevant to the discussion of the rationality of theism. Unfortunately it is not possible to separate the importance of a belief from the question of its truth. If there is a God, it seems important that one should believe that there is; but if there is not, is it so important to believe this? As we shall see later, the introduction of considerations of importance complicates the assessment of rationality; but the quest for rationality does not enable us to bypass the question of truth. We shall next consider this in the context of the justification of theism.

3

The Defensibility of Theism

IN THIS third lecture I at last attempt to come to grips
with the principal problems in the philosophy of
religion. The years since the second world war until
comparatively recently were a fairly sorry time for philosophy of religion in English speaking countries. It
was the period of the rise of linguistic philosophy
which was often confused with positivism in the minds
of theologians. The rise of this philosophy convinced
a number of philosophers that the traditional notion
of God was meaningless or self contradictory. Some
theologians concluded: "So much the worse for the
concept of God" and attempted to devise a religious
atheism; some drew the conclusion "so much the worse
for the notion of self-contradiction" and glorified ab-
surdity with the claim that God was above logic. Neither spectacle was edifying. Those theists who resisted
these follies remained on the defensive. Atheist philosophers of religion were more self-confident but not
more fertile. A chapter of A. J. Ayer's youthful work
Language, Truth, and Logic and four pages by Antony

Flew on theology and falsification called forth a hundred articles of defensive commentary and tentative refutation. Not since the time of Voltaire have the godly been set on a stir with so little outlay. But the criteria of meaningfulness which Ayer and Flew used to attack theology were, by the end of the seventies, no longer taken seriously, unless by a few theologians. In recent years there has been a revival of interest in philosophy of religion and a return of self-confidence among theistic philosophers.

The time has come to apply our criteria of rationality to the question whether the existence of God can be rationally believed. We will first ask whether it falls into one of our three categories of properly basic belief, and if it does not, we can inquire whether it is something that can be derived in the appropriate manner from beliefs that are properly basic.

Does the existence of God belong in the category of things that are self-evident or fundamental? Distinguished philosophers have thought that the proposition that God exists could be shown to be self-evident. Even the fool who says in his heart that there is no God, St. Anselm says, has an idea of God as a being than which no greater can be conceived. But a being than which no greater can be conceived must exist in reality as well as in idea, since to exist in reality is something greater than to exist merely in idea. Descartes also argued that since God was the most perfect being, and existence was a perfection, God must exist. An argument of this kind, which starts from the concept of God, or the meaning of the word "God," and attempts to show on that basis alone that God exists, is called an ontological argument. Philosophers as distinguished as Aquinas and Kant have endeavored to show that no ontological argument of this kind can be valid, so that the existence of God cannot be rendered self-evident. When I first came to philosophy some twenty years ago, the ontological argument was regarded as one of the deadest of all philosophical arguments: everyone agreed it was invalid, though there was not similar unanimous agreement as to *why* it was invalid. In the last two decades there have been ingenious and spirited attempts to revive it. I believe that they have failed, and that Aquinas and Kant were right to say that the existence of God is not self-evident.

If it is not self-evident, is the proposition that God exists something that is fundamental, in the sense of being something that is accepted as basic by all those who have an opinion on the matter? There is no doubt that it is possible for an individual to accept the existence of God as basic, and it seems very probable that there have been times and places where the proposition was accepted as basic by whole societies. In the Middle Ages in Europe, for example, the existence of God was probably a basic proposition for the overwhelming majority of believers; this was so even though during the same period it was believed that there existed valid proofs of the existence of God which might be useful in reasoning with unbelievers. But on the other hand it is equally clear that the existence of a God with attributes resembling those of the God of Western theism is not something which has been universally believed by the human race: quite apart from atheists in secular Western societies the adherents of many religions have not been monotheists, and the adherents of some—notably Buddhist—religions are not unequivocally describable as theists at all. Is it even the case that all those who have believed in the existence of the God of Judaism and Christianity and Islam have done so as something basic? I think not. There are many cases in which converts to theism report themselves as having been brought to believe in the existence of God by reasoning and argument. The arguments which converts report as having convinced them may or may not have been sound; but I see no reason to deny their claim that their belief has those reasons as its basis. Others who have been brought up to believe in God, and acquired their belief in the way that basic beliefs are acquired, may well have come at some point to question the belief, to consider the reasons for and against it, and eventually settled down to retain the belief on the basis of that reasoned consideration. It cannot be claimed with any plausibility that all those who believe in the existence of God hold it as a basic belief.

Nor does belief in the existence of God have the kind of unshakability characteristic of fundamental beliefs: it is not the kind of belief which can only be called into question by something which calls itself into question. No doubt there could be a society in which the existence of God, or of gods, was deeply embedded in everyone's noetic structure in such a way as to be implicit in every kind of inquiry: a society in which the main way in which people tried to find out about future or distant events was by consulting an oracle; in which all trials were carried out by ordeal; in which all cures were carried out by invocation, exorcism, or magic. In such a society, to question the existence of the divine would be to cast doubt on all accepted investigation and diagnosis. But it would only be if all societies were thus that the existence of God could be a fundamental truth in the sense I have defined.

With us, certainly, it is not so. The most earnest believers, in general, do not bring reference to God into their every day or scientific inquiry. Even those who pray to St. Anthony to help them find lost keys search their bureau drawers and turn out their pockets in the same way as the rest of us; Chemistry is taught by the same experiments in parochial schools as in nonreligious schools. In the universities God is not mentioned in the scientific textbooks which Christians share with atheists, nor in the project descriptions accompanying requests for research grants. Nor is this something which believers regard as a weakness in their believing in God, a sinful halfheartedness in their religious commitment.

I am not saying that there may not be conflicts between science and religion: there may well be particular issues—e.g., the creation of the world—where the dominant theories in one of the sciences may clash with the dominant interpretation of what is claimed as a religious revelation. What I am claiming is that even where there is an overlap, and a potential clash, between science and revealed religion, this is a clash between two distinct belief systems: the religion is not built into the procedures of scientific inquiry as it would be in the primitive culture that I imagined.

I am aware that even among religious people in our own society who broadly accept the methods and conclusions of contemporary scientific disciplines there are disagreements about the extent to which an appeal to divine intervention is necessary to explain what actually happens in the world. Some Christian men of science operate with a deist model: in creating the world, God sets up for all a set of natural laws, and the initial conditions upon which these laws operate; all that happens thenceforth (with the possible exception of human choices) is determined by these laws and these initial conditions. Events in history are God's acts only insofar as they are the consequences of this single creative action; if any events are to be specially ascribed to God this can only be because they are miraculous interruptions of the course of nature initially laid down.

There is another view according to which many things are left undetermined by natural laws; not only human actions and decisions, but such things as the course of the weather. Here there is room in history for divine action which is neither the initial determining of the laws which govern our universe, nor yet an intervention in the operation of those laws occurring by way of miracle. But even those who hold this latter view do not regard recourse to God as a method of scientific inquiry: rather they believe the contingent nature of some events within the purview of science sets limits to the possibility of scientific explanation by such sciences as meteorology, economics, psychology. Belief in the contingency of the weather will not affect the methods of a practising meteorologist: though it may affect the decisions of those who pray for rain or sunshine.

We cannot, then, place belief in the existence of God in the category of fundamental beliefs.

Can we locate the existence of God in the second ✓ 2. category of properly basic beliefs—those that are evident to the senses or memory? This reduces to the question whether the existence of God can become evident to the senses. It was necessary, for completeness, to add the category of those that are evident to memory as a category of basic beliefs; but though not everything which is evident to memory is evident to the senses, only what can be evident to the senses can be evident to memory, in the use of "memory" which is appropriate when we are talking about the use of "I remember it" to justify a claim to know, or an expression of belief in something.

Memory, we might want to say, is an intellectual as well as a sensory capacity: we can remember a priori truths as well as things we have seen & heard. But to remember something intellectually is simply to have learned it and not yet forgotten it: here, remembering it is just still knowing (believing) it; and to say "I remember" is simply to reaffirm, not to justify, the claim to know. Whereas, the sensory memory is a source of justification of basic beliefs.

Of course, one can remember something without remembering the sense-experience at the time of what is remembered: I can remember a fact without being able to remember whether I saw it happen, heard it happen, or was merely told about it later. But only what can be sensed can be remembered in the appropriate use of "remember." So if someone claims to know that God exists because it is evident to his memory then, unless he subscribes to the Platonic thesis that we can remember things that happened to us in a previous nonbodily experience, he is claiming to have had an experience which made the existence of God "manifest to the senses." Is this possible?

If God is an immaterial spirit, and has no body, however ethereal, then God cannot literally be seen with the ordinary senses. Visions of God, such as those attributed to Moses in the Bible, must at best be regarded as the seeing of a miraculous manifestation or symbol of God, not as a literal seeing of an invisible divinity. Even those who take such accounts with the greatest seriousness and reverence usually see them as having the role of a special communication or revelation of himself by God to a favored servant, rather than as something related to belief in God's existence in the way in which our occasional fleeting sightings of Halley's comet provide evidence for its existence.

The way in which it is popular to claim that the existence of God has the same status as those beliefs which are manifest to the senses is rather this. Some people have, and perhaps all people can have, religious experiences; and religious experiences put us in contact with God. It is true that God, since He has no body, cannot be perceived by the external senses, but we (or at least some of us) have an inner sense which can be trained to focus on God and thus provide irrefutable evidence of His existence.

I think that the expression "religious experience" is an unfortunate one; not because of anything to do with religion, but because of the confusing nature of the relevant concept of "experience." The word is used to cover any item in a person's mental history, whether sense-experience, feeling, emotions, imaginations, dreams and reveries. It thus provides a catchall which includes items of very diverse cognitive status. In particular "religious experience" includes many different kinds of things from the most exalted states of those far advanced in mystical pursuits to the sentiments shared by any less than totally hardhearted participant in a religious wedding or funeral.

Sentiments of grief, of guilt, of justification, forgiveness, and exaltation in the context of a religious liturgy or on the occasion of the reading of a sacred text clearly play an important and valued part in the life of a religious believer. The unbeliever may despise them or he may envy them: he can hardly deny their existence or their significance in the lives of those who have them. He may see a distant analogy to them in his own life in the way in which he is moved by reading great literature or stirred by attending or participating in dramatic, musical, and operatic performances. He may find a closer, nonreligious analogy in the sentiments of patriotic citizens at solemn commemorations of national events, or in the emotions of the happily married on attending the wedding of a young couple. On the basis of these analogies he is likely to judge that religious experience in this sense cannot be a basis for belief in God. The sentiments get their significance and profundity from the institutions which provide their context, and not vice-versa. They are not related to these institutions as evidence is to hypothesis. It would be as absurd to argue from the vividness of liturgical exaltation to the existence of God as it would be to argue from the emotion generated by King Lear that he must have existed, to argue from the patriotic fervor one feels at a military parade to the justice of one's country's cause, or from the fond feelings watching newly taken marriage vows to the validity or stability of one's own marriage. We do not argue to truth of Nazism from fervor of Nuremberg rallies; we condemn that fervor because of what we know of Nazism. So in general: we judge the institution to find out what value to put on the fervor it enshrines and unlocks. We do not regard the fervor as justifying the goals and self-descriptions of the institutions. I conclude that religious experience, in the sense of sentiment embedded in religious institutions, cannot make the existence of God manifest to the senses.

What of the rather different kinds of experience claimed by the mystics? Can the experience of mystics be regarded as a perception of God with a secret, interior, sensory capacity? The notion of an "inner sense" has been popular in the history of philosophy, but it is as confusing as the concept of "experience." Many philosophers have regarded the operation of the memory and the imagination as being one kind of inward sense. The implicit comparison with the external senses is misleading.

The external senses—e.g., the five senses of sight, sound, touch, taste, smell—are all discriminatory capacities: e.g., sight is the capacity to tell light from dark, colors from each other; with touch we can tell hot from cold, one shape from another, and so on; with taste we distinguish sweet from sour, cherries from garlic, and so on. For the exercise of each of the senses we have to be in a particularly bodily relationship—differing in a characteristic way from sense to sense—with the object to be sensed: we have to have the cherries in our mouths, turn our head in the right direction to see the star, etc. The senses have organs: that is to say, to each modality of sense-perception there is related a part of the body which can be voluntarily manipulated in ways which affect the operation of the sense: as we turn our heads to listen, feel the shape of something with our hands, open our eyes to see, and so on.

It is these elementary and obvious facts about the senses which mean that their operation is something that can be checked up on and followed by other people. It is these which make sense-perception a public activity that can be shared by others: many of us can look at the same object, hear the same sounds, and so on. These elementary facts are ignored by philosophers who want to talk about imagination and memory as inner senses. To the general incoherence of the notion of an inner sense, there are special difficulties to be added when we consider the idea that God might be perceived by an inner sense.

I have already rejected the idea that God can be perceived by an inner sense of memory independent of the exterior senses. Could we say that the existence of God might be discovered by the exercise of the imagination? The imagination is clearly not a means of acquiring information about the world outside us in the way that the senses are. One cannot discover the way the world is by simply imagining. Nonetheless there is a sense in which we can increase our knowledge of things by using our imagination. It is similar to the way in which we can learn to see things better by drawing them or modeling them. Using our imagination can increase our sensitivity to other people and thus our ability to inform ourselves about what they feel and are likely to do. Works of the imagination may teach us things about human beings; great works of fiction are means by which the human race extends its self-awareness. Could we say that knowledge of God could be acquired by the use of the imagination, in the way our knowledge of ourselves and of our peers grows through storytelling and poetry?

For imagination to be a genuine source of knowledge there has to be some way of distinguishing what is discovered by the imagination from what is created by the imagination. How can we settle whether God is discovered by the imagination or created by it? After all, if there is no God, then God is incalculably the greatest single creation of the human imagination. No other creation of the imagination has been so fertile of ideas, so great an inspiration to philosophy, to literature, to painting, sculpture, architecture, and drama. Set beside the idea of God, the most original inventions of mathematicians and the most unforgettable characters in drama are minor products of the imagination: Hamlet and the square root of minus one pale into insignificance by comparison. But the very fact that an atheist can salute the idea of God as a magnificent work of the human imagination shows that whether God really exists is something which the imagination itself cannot settle. The apparatus of the human mind described by Freud (to take another example) is something whose description does credit to Freud's imaginative genius; but whether it really describes the human mind in a scientific way, or is a newly created mythology, is something which has to be settled outside the realm of the imagination.

Some think that mystics perceive God by a special inner sense, whose object is the divine in the way that sight has light and dark and color for its object. I do not wish to deny the importance of mystical experience; nor have I any confidence that I can give any adequate account or explanation of it. But I do feel confident that it is misrepresented if it is described as experience of God.

If there is a God with the attributes ascribed to him by Western theism, then he is everlasting, unchanging, and ubiquitous. In relation to such an object there cannot be any activity of discrimination resembling the discriminatory activities of the senses: we cannot have a sixth sense which detects that God is here and not there, as we can see that something is red at one end and not at another, or which detects that God was a moment ago and is not now, as we can hear a noise which suddenly stops. If God is everywhere always, there can be no sense to discriminate the places and times where he is from those where he is not; the whole nature of a sense is an ability to tell differences of this kind. A sense of God would be as absurd as a sense of sight whose only function was to detect a uniform unchanging whiteness or a sense of hearing whose only function was to listen to a single unchanging middle C. Seeing whiteness only makes sense amid telling one color from another; hearing middle C involves telling it from other notes. One cannot get nearer to or get further from God as one can get nearer to or further from a source of light or sound: one cannot be too early or too late to encounter him as one might be to see or hear something. The whole context within which talk of sense-experience makes sense is lacking in the case of alleged sense-experience of God.

Mystics themselves are as willing to describe mystical experiences in terms of unity of will with God as they are in cognitive terms. But whether the union with God is described in terms of love, or compared with a seeing, or a touching, or a tasting of godhead, it cannot be taken literally as the operation of a sixth sense. For the mode of operation of the alleged faculty differs too much from the mode of operation of genuine senses; and the essential attributes of the alleged object to be sensed differ too greatly from the attributes of any possible object of sensory discrimination.

Those who wish to attribute cognitive value to mystical experiences, whether reached through traditional forms of religious discipline, or allegedly secured by the shortcut of drugs, do better to present mysticism as a nonsensory method of acquiring information than as an extraordinary sense in its own right. But in that case mysticism is seen as a mode of revelation of the divine; and under that description I will consider it in the next lecture. For the present I shall take it as established that the existence of mystical experiences cannot justify the acceptance of the existence of God as basic in the same way as we are justified in accepting as basic those truths which are manifest to the senses.

If the existence of God cannot be accepted as basic in either of the first two categories of properly basic belief, it remains to be seen whether it can be rationally held as basic because it is defensible by argument or inquiry or performance. If this is so, then those who accept the existence of God as something basic may be acting well within their epistemic rights, but only if they can present to others a defense of their belief either by offering arguments or by inquiry, or in some way analogous to justification by performance.

The position that basic belief in the existence of God is defensible in this way has a long history in natural theology. Thomas Aquinas, for instance, though he thought that the existence of God was demonstrable by argument, considered that it was properly held as basic by most believers because of the possibility of offering rational argument in its defense. If this is so, there will be evidence for the existence of God, but it will not be playing the role of evidence in relation to most believers, because for them it will itself be as evident, as well-known, as anything which could be offered in evidence for it.

If the existence of God is to be something justifiably held as basic, this will entail that it will be something which can be defended by argument or by inquiry or in some other way. It will be justifiable if any of the traditional arguments for the existence of God can be shown to be sound, and if the traditional arguments against the existence of God can be shown to be invalid.

When I described the forms by which basic beliefs can be shown to be defensible, I listed argument, inquiry, and performance. The category of things defensible by inquiry is not an important one when it is the justification of theism that we have in mind. If there is evidence for the existence of God, it is evidence which is available for everyone. The starting points of traditional proofs of the existence of God have not been recondite facts which only professional men know and which only scientific enterprise could discover. They have been things which everybody knows, as that some things move, or that some things pass out of existence, or that there are relations of cause and effect in the world. But we should look for a moment at the third category of defensible basic beliefs, those which are defensible by performance. A water diviner, I suggested, who has a good record at finding water, is justified in his belief that there is water where the hazel switch twitches in his hand, though neither he nor anyone knows the mechanism, if any, by which he discovers water. I do not, however, think that this provides justification for anyone else to hold as basic the belief that there is water where the dowser says so; on the contrary, anyone else who believes it is doing so—rationally enough—on the basis of an inductive argument from the good track record. Performance provides justification for a basic belief only for the actual performer.

Now who, if anyone, is the relevant performer when the belief in question is belief in the existence of God? One might suggest that the relevant performers are the saints, holy people, those who have led holy lives; perhaps those who prophesy, work miracles, heal the sick. Most saints would regard it, I think, as impious to say that their belief in the existence of God could be justified by pointing to the holiness of their own lives. Even those who work miracles of healing are, after all, *faith* healers; that is to say, the healing is allegedly performed on the basis of the faith. The faith is the precondition of the healing, not something which is justified, to themselves, by the success of the healing. The attitude of mind which would look for such a justification would itself be an impoverishment of the necessary faith. A faith healer may well point to his cures as a reason why others should believe; but if that is the case the belief is being demanded on the basis of the healer's testimony to the content of the belief, and the miracles are being pointed to as the justification of the authority of the witness.

I conclude, then, that belief in the existence of God as a basic belief is something which is justifiable and defensible only if traditional natural theology is a possible discipline, that is to say, if the traditional activity of offering evidence for the existence of God and arguments against disproofs of the existence of God can be successfully carried out.

Interest in the question of the rationality of the belief in the existence of God often originates from a desire to short-circuit the forbidding task of examining the arguments for and against the existence of God. If I am right, there cannot be any such general short-cut. Individuals may believe in the existence of God as something basic, but they are rationally justified in doing so only if it is in general possible to offer sound arguments for the existence of God and to refute arguments against it.

I shall turn in the next and final lecture to whether belief in the existence of God can be rational if it is accepted not as something basic but as something which is derived from something basic. Obviously, if it is accepted on the basis of argument and those arguments are themselves valid and sound then the belief is rational. What is a much more interesting and difficult question is whether belief in God can be valid if based on testimony, and that takes us to the final topic of faith. The world is full of people who offer to bear witness that there is a God and to bear witness that he has planned the salvation, redemption, and judgment of the world. The question of the final lecture is how the rational person should react to that witness, how do we respond rationally without falling into either of the vice of skepticism or that of credulity.

The Virtue of Faith

IN THE last lecture I considered belief in the existence of God, and claimed that it could not be rationally accepted as basic on the ground that it was self-evident or fundamental, or that it was manifest to any sense interior or exterior. If it can be rationally believed in as basic, that is because it is defensible by argument or inquiry. If traditional natural theology is a viable enterprise theism is defensible by argument, and thus belief in God is rational, even if held as basic. Whether traditional natural theology *can* be successfully pursued is a large topic to which in these lectures I could not hope to do justice, so that I must content myself with this modest, conditional conclusion.

Can the existence of God be known by testimony? It might be thought that testimony could not be an ultimate source of information: it cannot add to the patrimony of human knowledge, but only circulate existing capital from mind to mind. I do not think this is entirely true: in some areas—the existence of customs and practices, for instance—testimony may be our only source of evidence. But testimony could be given to the existence of God only by reporting experiences of God (and these we have denied to be possible) or arguments to establish God's existence (which will be effective only if natural theology can be successful). The role of testimony in religious belief is not in connection with the existence of God, but in relation to revelation from God. It makes claims, not on belief in God, but on faith in God.

In the theological tradition in which I was brought up faith was contrasted on the one hand with reason and knowledge, and on the other with hope and charity. "Faith" was used in a narrower sense than "belief." Aristotle believed, and perhaps believed with good reason, that there was a divine prime mover unmoved; but his belief was not, according to this tradition, faith in God. So not all belief in God was faith in God. On the other hand, not all faith in God was charity or love of God. Marlowe's Faustus, when he speaks of Christ's blood streaming in the firmament, has long ceased to love God above all things and has no further hope of salvation; yet he retains a belief in the saving value of Christ's death which is faith and not knowledge. He lacks the other theological virtues of hope and charity, but he retains the theological virtue of faith. It is this "theological virtue" which is the principal topic of this lecture: faith, which is a special kind of belief on theological topics, yet not a belief so special as to find expression in a loving service of God. This is the kind of faith which has often been contrasted with reason. I want to ask now whether faith of this kind is a rational frame of mind, and whether it is, as theologians have claimed, a genuine virtue.

The special nature of the belief that is faith is that it is a belief in something as revealed by God; belief in a proposition on the word of God. Faith, thus defined, is a correlate of revelation; for faith to be possible it must be possible to identify something as the word of God.

In the tradition of which I am speaking the relationship between faith and reason was expounded as follows. It was possible to know, by unaided natural reason, without any appeal to a supernatural revelation, that there is a God. Equally it was possible to know by natural reason certain things about him, as that he was almighty, all-knowing, incapable of deceit, a rewarder of those who lived a good life and a punisher of those who lived badly. Again, it was possible to learn, without appealing to any premise which was not ascertainable and defensible by plain reason, that God has revealed to the human race certain truths about himself which were not ascertainable by reason. The truths which it was alleged had been thus revealed were of various kinds: that Israel was God's chosen people, that there were three persons in one God, that the Eucharist was Christ's body and blood, that the Holy Spirit does not desert the elect, that the wicked would suffer forever in Hell. Those who agreed that there was a divine revelation which called for faith might disagree on the particular content of the revelation.

Equally, there were many different forms in which the revelation might be made, different channels by which it reached the human race from God—perhaps through Moses or the prophets, perhaps through Christ, or the Bible, or the Church, or even in an enlightenment of the individual conscience. What was common to all these different cases was that the believer's faith was belief in certain propositions as having been specially revealed by God. Because the propositions were not demonstrable without appeal to revelation, because they were indeed opaque and might appear repugnant to the unaided human intelligence, faith in these propositions differed from reason. But because the fact of their being revealed could be proved, it was claimed, beyond rational cavil, faith was not in conflict with reason but was a rational state of mind. Faith was a virtue permitting the mind access to truths which would otherwise be beyond its reach.

Faith, so conceived, had a number of important properties. It was intellectual, opaque, rational, free, gratuitous, and certain. It was intellectual in the sense that it was capable of articulation in language: it was not intellectual in the sense of being cold and unemotional (indeed living faith, as contrasted with dead faith, would be alive with love of God and of one's neighbor). But the possibility of articulation in language was a crucial feature of faith: it was indeed the language in which one's state of mind found expression which decided whether one's state of mind was the virtue of faith or the opposed vice of infidelity or heresy, depending on whether it was in accord with creeds and scripture.

Faith was opaque in the sense that at least some of the propositions in which it found expression were incapable of being seen to be true by an intellectual process which did not appeal to the occurrence of a divine revelation. Moreover, at least some of its propositions were so difficult to understand as to be apparently incoherent—they were, in the technical term, "mysteries" of faith.

Despite being mysterious, faith was rational because publicly ascertainable data existed which provided good reasons for believing that the content of the creeds and scriptures and the authoritative beliefs of the religious community had been revealed by God. The content of revelation was beyond reason's power to reach, but the fact of revelation was something which unaided reason could ascertain.

Though faith was rational faith was also free. That is to say, there was no necessity of nature, nothing in logic or in the makeup of the human mind, which forced any human being to believe, or prevented him from disbelieving. Faith was free, not in the sense that it was optional—it might be required under pain of damnation—but that it was the object of a free choice on the part of the believer.

Faith was gratuitous in the sense that it was a gift

of divine grace. That is to say, in the causal explanation of why some people believed and others did not there must enter as an essential element the free decision of God choosing the individuals to believe. This decision was free and one which God could have refrained from making: not just in the sense that so to refrain would be, so to speak, part of his omnipotent repertoire, but also in the sense that no injustice or impropriety would be involved in such a decision.

Finally, faith was certain: it involved a commitment without reserve to the articles of faith; a resolve to disregard evidence conflicting with them. In this, faith was a state of mind resembling knowledge. In the case of faith as in the case of knowledge there might be reasons of a pastoral or academic kind for examining conflicting evidence; but for a true believer there can never be a question of examining conflicting evidence with a view to possible revision of one's commitment to the articles of faith.

So far I have been concerned simply to expound a particular tradition concerning the relation between faith and reason. This tradition I have summed up by saying that according to it faith is intellectual, opaque, rational, free, gratuitous, and certain. Other traditions give different accounts. I have expounded this one not simply because it is the one most familiar to me but also because it is the one which was most explicitly articulated to safeguard the concerns of reason, and therefore the one which it is most appropriate to evaluate when we wish to ask whether faith is a rational frame of mind. Let us now turn from exposition to critical evaluation.

If A believes a certain proposition p on the word of God, there are three principal questions which arise. First, what is the relation between A's belief that God exists and his belief that p? Second, what is the relation between A's belief that p and A's belief that God has revealed that p? Third, what is the relation between A's belief that God has revealed that p and the historical events that A could point to to justify this belief?

First of all, it seems that faith must presuppose belief in the existence of God. If faith is belief that a proposition is true because God has revealed it, it does not seem possible that one could have faith in the existence of God. When somebody has faith that p, his reason for believing that p is that God has revealed that p. As we have seen in the first lecture, p cannot be offered as a reason for q unless it is better known than q; and p cannot be better known than q if it is impossible to know p without knowing q, or impossible to believe p without believing q. It does not seem possible that someone could believe that God had revealed something without believing that God existed.

I do not deny that one and the same event might provide grounds both for believing that God existed and for believing that he had revealed something. Suppose that the stars were to wheel in their courses and to spell out the sentence: "The end of the world is at hand." This would, no doubt, provide reason both for believing that God existed (who else would be powerful enough to control the stars?) and that the end of the world was at hand. I do not say the reason would necessarily be overwhelming. An atheist would, if he thought that was what he saw, no doubt wish to explore other avenues of inquiry before falling on his knees (is it really the stars, or has NASA discovered some new way of producing celestial pyrotechnics?); and even a theist might be in doubt what to think if the message spelt out had been something different, such as "Drink Coca-Cola" or "Give ear to the Reverend Moon": is there a powerful demon at work, perhaps, mocking the faithful? Still, such an event would provide a reason for believing in God and believing in the imminent end of the world, even if the reason is not necessarily overwhelming. But in such a case it would be the mode of production of the sentence which would establish the existence of God and the content of the sentence which would reveal the approach of the final days. It would not be a case of believing in the existence of God because God has revealed it, not even if the message spelled out in the skies was "I am the Lord thy God."

To say that one could not believe God exists because God has revealed it is not to make any criticism of the traditional account of faith which I expounded. It was no part of that tradition that the believer's belief in the existence of God was itself part of the theological virtue of faith. It was however taught that given the minimal belief in a deity capable of self-revelation, the most fundamental truths about the divinity (e.g., that there is only one God and that He created the world) may in many cases be believed on faith, even though they are naturally ascertainable and can be accepted as a result of rational inquiry.

It follows that it is a precondition of the acceptability of the traditional account of faith and reason that the existence of God is something that can be known or rationally believed. It is not necessary that each believer should have a state of mind which could strictly be called "knowledge" that God exists. To return to the kind of considerations aired in the first lecture: the little astronomical information I possess could hardly be called "knowledge" by any strict test; much of it is no doubt hazy misinformation, and even in cases where I am quite confident that I am in the right (as in my belief that Venus is farther away from us than the moon is) I would find it very hard to give a proof which would convince a skeptic. Yet my belief that Venus is farther away from us than the moon is a rational belief because there are other people who know that it is, and I have a good idea where to find them and how I can learn from them.

In the same way many people have believed in God's existence because they were brought up to do so rather than because they had reasons for doing so that would convince an unbeliever. This does not make their belief, and the faith of which it is a precondition, necessarily irrational. It will not do so as long as there are people—theologians and philosophers say—who can if the need arises expound to them reasons for believing in God and the existence and role of these experts is known by the believers.

Such is the account given of the condition of "simple believers" by a theologian such as Thomas Aquinas. This part of his account of the nature of faith does not present difficulty: it accords with the conclusions we reached, from a different viewpoint, about the propriety of holding a belief as basic provided that it was defensible by argument and inquiry. The state of mind of the "simple believer" is not knowledge, except in the loose sense in which I can talk of my "knowledge" of astronomy; but it is reasonable belief. Depending on the circumstances of the individual case it may either be basic defensible belief, or nonbasic belief on the testimony of those more expert in natural theology. Always provided, that is, that natural theology is a venture that can be successfully carried out.

I turn to the second question: the relationship between believing p and believing that God has revealed that p. One might well ask: if one believes that God has revealed that p, how can one fail to believe that p? When other people tell us things, we may or may not believe them. Believing someone is not just believing what they say: one might already believe it, or come to see it as true for oneself; it is not just believing something on the strength of their saying so (he may be a habitual liar who always gets things wrong; so when he says that p, I believe that p, because I know he is both misinformed and intending to deceive). It is to trust someone's word for something. Human beings we may mistrust, but how could anyone in their senses mistrust the word of God, who can neither deceive nor be mistaken?

Aquinas maintained that however certain one might be that God had revealed that p, one's belief that p would not amount to knowledge even if one were absolutely correct in believing that God had so revealed. This was because one's opinion about p would be based on an extrinsic criterion rather than on insight into the matter in question. This seems implausible: perhaps Aquinas' opinion was due to excessive deference to a theory of knowledge put forward in the *Posterior Analytics* of Aristotle; or perhaps he was worried that if the believer's state of mind with regard to the mysteries of faith could be regarded as knowledge, faith would no longer be subject to freedom. But this too seems to rest on a misconception of the nature of knowledge: it is all too easy to shut one's mind to what one knows. But it is in fact very unlikely that someone would believe that God had revealed that p, and not believe that p, though he might try to forget it. What is much more likely is that doubt about p will carry with it doubt about whether p had really been revealed by God.

The real problem concerning the relation between the belief in an article of faith and the belief that God has revealed it turns on the degree of commitment involved in each belief. Faith, as was mentioned earlier, involves certainty: it is a commitment which is comparable to the commitment which a person has to the propositions which he claims to know. Now is it possible for the belief to have that degree of certainty unless the belief in the fact of revelation has the same certainty? If not, can it be claimed that belief in the fact of a revelation can be rationally held with that degree of certainty? If not, can faith itself be rational?

It is sometimes argued that faith is vicious, because it is a commitment appropriate only to the knowledge in the absence of the kind of basis which would justify a claim to knowledge. I have in the past used this argument myself. Reflection on the kinds of considerations spelled out in the earlier lectures has convinced me that the argument will not do. It is wrong to say that one cannot have a commitment to the truth of a proposition as strong as the commitment that goes with knowledge, unless knowledge is present. The fundamental propositions are all held with a degree of commitment as strong as any knowledge claim could carry with it, and yet they are not known in the sense of being supported by justifying reasons. So if faith is vicious, it is not because it is certainty unaccompanied by knowledge.

However, all the cases which convinced me, and I hope convinced you, that there could be justified certainty without knowledge, were cases where the certainty, the unshakable belief, was not one based on reasons. The reason why the certainty was justified in the absence of the reasons was that the beliefs in question were more certain, were better known than, any reasons on which they might be held. It was precisely because they would have been more certain than any reasons offered that we said they could not be based on reason; because a reason cannot be less certain than that for which it is offered as a reason.

The arguments we considered earlier showed that it can be rational to believe something with greater firmness than one believes any of the reasons one could offer in support of it, as I believe in the existence of Australia with greater firmness than in any of the reasons I might offer to convince somebody geographically ignorant. But the arguments do not show that one can rationally believe p for the reason that q with a commitment stronger than one's commitment to q. The arguments all concerned cases where it is appropriate to say that p is not, or no longer, believed for reasons.

But this does nothing to solve the difficulty which we have just raised about the degree of commitment involved in faith. For faith is by definition a belief in something for a particular reason: namely, that God has revealed it. Since the alleged divine revelation is the reason for the belief in the article of faith p, one cannot rationally believe p on faith with a stronger commitment than that of one's belief that God has revealed that p. The crucial question, then, is whether this can be believed rationally with the unshakable commitment faith demands.

Belief in a divine revelation has two elements: first,

that there is a God who can reveal himself; second, that certain historical events constitute an actual revelation. The first is something which we have agreed can rationally be believed as basic, if it is defensible, say, by natural theology. But can it be believed not only as basic but as unshakably certain? This is something which we have not shown any reason to believe. Ought the belief not to be accompanied with a degree of reserve and caution? And if so will it not be inadequate to provide a foothold for faith? Yet we have already agreed that there can be some beliefs held as basic, which it is rational to hold unshakably, even though they are not fundamental in the sense of being rationally accepted by all who accept them. Might the existence of God be one of these?

Whether this was so or not would depend on the form of the proof of the existence of God which established the defensibility of theism. If it were the kind of proof which showed that the existence of God was, as St. Paul thought, something so obvious that only ill will could doubt it, then the answer to our question would be yes. It might be thought that if something were obvious, a philosophical proof would be neither possible or necessary. But this need not be so. Philosophers have doubted whether there are bodies external to the mind, and whether there exist minds other than their own; other philosophers have offered proofs of the existence of the external world and of other minds. But the existence of bodies and of human beings other than myself is so obvious that the only form a "proof" of their existence could really take would be an exposure of the sophistries in the arguments on the other side; arguments which tend to throw doubt on, or interpret away, the obvious truths that I see other bodies and talk to other people. Arguments for the existence of God cannot be quite on the same footing, since nobody literally sees God or talks with God; but they might have the form of showing that there is something sophistical in any of the arguments which seek to cast doubt on the efficacy of the naive theist's conclusion that there must be a God because the world must have been made by somebody. Whether the natural theologian can succeed in doing this is a large and difficult question; I leave it aside as I am leaving aside the more general question whether the existence of God can be proved in any manner. I turn instead to the second part or element of the belief that a revelation has taken place, that certain historical events are to be interpreted as a communication from God.

The question how events can be interpreted as a communication from God is a difficult one: but I want to consider first the prior difficulty: how is it known that the events in question took place at all? According to the traditional view of the nature of faith, events such as the lives and sayings of Jesus and Moses, and the decisions of authoritative organs of the religious communities, are known by the ordinary methods of historical inquiry.

But if this is so, do not the considerations which

enabled us to defend faith against being a conviction appropriate only to knowledge in the absence of knowledge provide a difficulty for the justification of the belief in revelation? For the belief in the fact of revelation has to share the certain commitment of the belief in the article of faith itself; but the belief in the fact of revelation involves belief in propositions based on straightforward historical evidence. So the question is now raised: can the historical facts be known with a certainty which justifies a commitment as strong as that of faith?

This question is partly a philosophical question and partly a historical question. The philosophical question is whether there are *any* facts of history which call for a belief of this degree of commitment. The answer to the philosophical question seems to be clearly yes. I believe that Hitler existed with the same kind of commitment that I believe that Australia exists; the belief is basic in the same way in that it is more evident to me than anything I could offer others by way of evidence in favor of it; and it is unshakable in the same way in that anything which was offered as evidence against it would call its own evidential value in question. And in addition to basic unshakable historical truths of this kind, there are others which I would claim to know (as that Cicero was once consul of Rome, and that Charles I was beheaded in London).

Now are there facts interpretable as a divine revelation which are known with this degree of certainty? Whether there are facts in the life of the founders of

the great religions which are known in the strict sense
is a matter for the historian rather than the philosopher to answer; but I would myself not regard as rash
a claim to know that Moses led an exodus of Israelites
from Egypt, and that Jesus was crucified, and perhaps
that the night before he died he took bread and said
"this is my body." Can the same be said of all those
events in their histories which are pointed to by their
followers as the justification for the belief that their
characteristic doctrines are divinely revealed? I very
much doubt it. No doubt it may be reasonably believed that Moses and Jesus did & said many of the
things ascribed to them in the Bible; but can it reasonably be believed with a degree of certainty resembling
that of knowledge? Unless the relevant stories can be
as certain as the commitment which faith demands of
the believer, the commitment is, so far forth as it is
faith, irrational; and if the belief is a commitment
which is rationally in proportion to the support given
by the history, it is, so far forth as it is rational, something less than faith.

Someone may, of course, believe that the Bible is
a historically totally reliable account because he believes that it is the inspired word of God. He may believe this not on the grounds of ordinary historical
probability, but on the authority of the teaching of a
church which proclaims the inspiration and inerrancy
of the Bible. But if that is so, then he cannot in turn
derive the authority of the church from the authority
of the Bible considered as an inspired document: that

would be to argue in a circle. He can rest the belief in the authority of the church only on the Bible as it is judged by the historian; and that, if what we have just said is correct, is not strong enough to bear the weight of an irrevocable commitment to everything that is contained in it, included whatever passages may be pointed to as the charter of the church in question.

I conclude, then, my inquiry into the rationality of faith with the conclusion that faith is not, as theologians have claimed, a virtue, but a vice, unless a number of conditions can be fulfilled. One of them is that the existence of God can be rationally justified outside faith. Secondly, whatever are the historical events which are pointed to as constituting the divine revelation must be independently established as historically certain with the degree of commitment which one can have in the pieces of historical knowledge of the kind I have mentioned.

I return finally to the question of the justification of belief in God, belief in the existence of God, as contrasted with faith. I realize that at the end of the last lecture I left this question in an unsatisfactory condition in saying that I thought that belief in the existence of God was justified only if natural theology could be carried out successfully, that is, if the arguments in favor of the existence of God were or could be made sound. I gave no answer to the question whether they can. The reason I gave no answer is that I do not know the answer. I do not myself know of any argument for the existence of God which I find convincing; in all of them I think I can find flaws. Equally I do not know of any argument against the existence of God which is totally convincing; in the arguments I know against the existence of God I can equally find flaws. So that my own position on the existence of God is agnostic.

I say "agnostic" deliberately, and not "atheist," because I think that the atheist no less than the theist has to scrutinize his beliefs to see to what extent they pass the test of rationality which I outlined at the beginning. It has been argued by Professor Flew that there is a presumption of atheism: in his book with that title, *The Presumption of Atheism,* he says that unless the proofs of the existence of God are valid then one should be an atheist because the burden of proof is on the theist. But his argument for a presumption of atheism does not succeed. Flew distinguishes between positive and negative atheists; a negative atheist is simply someone who is not a theist. Negative atheism, in his view, differs from agnosticism because agnosticism involves thinking it makes sense to say that God exists, and someone might not be a theist because he thought it did not make sense to say this. Flew then says there is a defensible presumption in favor of negative atheism.

I think it is correct to say that there is a presumption in favor of ignorance over knowledge: that is to say, it takes more effort to show that you do know something than it takes to show that you don't know something. But I do not know why one should call the position of ignorance—the position of not knowing whether there is a God, perhaps not knowing whether it even makes sense to say there is one—negative atheism. One could just as well have divided the field in the following way: a positive theist is someone who positively accepts the existence of God, and a negative theist is simply somebody who is not an atheist. In that case, by a simple redefinition, all Flew's arguments would establish a presumption of theism rather than a presumption of atheism—a presumption of negative theism, of course, but then, after all, it was only a presumption of negative atheism which he claimed to establish himself.

But if we drop Flew's insistence that an agnostic must be someone who positively thinks *God* is a coherent concept, rather than someone who does not know this, then the negative theist and the negative atheist are both better called agnostics. Now is there a presumption of agnosticism? Yes, there is, in the sense that it takes more to prove knowledge than to exhibit ignorance. But this methodological presumption, of course, does not necessarily let the agnostic off the hook. An examination candidate may be able to justify fully the claim not to know the answer to one of the questions set, but that won't get him through the examination.

I must return for the last time to the triad of rationality, skepticism and credulity from which I began. Both the theist and the atheist may well be erring on the side of credulity. The position is not that the atheist is more skeptical, necessarily, than the theist. It may well be the case, and indeed from an agnostic's view-point it is the case, that both the theist and the atheist are erring by being credulous. They are both believing something, the one a positive proposition, the other a negative proposition, in the absence of the appropriate justification. On the other hand, from the point of view of either the theist or the atheist, the agnostic is erring by skepticism, that is, he has no view on a topic on which he should have a view. In giving an account of the virtue of rationality, I said earlier, it was not enough to list each of one's beliefs and to see whether each of them passed the test of rational acceptability. Something else had to be considered, namely whether someone had beliefs at all on particular topics. This shows that there is something deceptive about the Aristotelian triad of the person who believes too much, the person who believes too little, and the person who believes the right amount. There is great truth in this, but what is misleading about it is that the criterion for erring on the one side is different from the criterion for erring on the other. You err on the side of credulity if you have a belief that does not fall into one of the categories of justified belief; you err on the side of skepticism, not by the same test, but by lacking a belief on a topic on which you should have a belief. And so the final question is whether it is the agnostic who is erring on the side of skepticism or the theist or atheist who is erring on the side of credulity.

At this point one has to make a distinction between necessary and contingent agnosticism. Necessary agnosticism is the belief which many philosophers such as Kant have had that knowledge whether there is a God or not is in some sense impossible because of the limits of the human mind. There are several philosophical arguments to the effect that agnosticism about the existence of God is something which is built into the human condition rightly understood. I find the arguments for that kind of agnosticism as unconvincing as either the arguments for theism or for atheism.

Contrasted with necessary agnosticism is the contingent agnosticism of a man who says: "I do not know whether there is a God, but perhaps it can be known; I have no proof that it cannot be known." Contingent agnosticism of that sort involves not knowing whether other people know, or only think they know, that there is a God. When I, from my agnostic viewpoint, look at my theist and atheist colleagues I do not know whether to envy them or pity them. Should I envy them for having a firm belief on a topic on which it is important to have a firm belief, and on which I myself have none? Should I pity them because of the flimsiness of the arguments and considerations which they use to justify their theism or atheism? From my viewpoint they appear as credulous; from their viewpoint, I appear as skeptical. Which of us is rational, I do not know. Whether this is my own tragedy, or part of the human condition, I do not know.

I have shared with you everything I know on the

topic of the relationship between faith and reason. On the really important matter, whether there is a God or not, I have nothing to share with you except my ignorance.

References

1. Plantinga, in C. F. Delaney, ed., *Rationality and Religious Belief* (Notre Dame, Ind.: University of Notre Dame Press, 1979). See also "Is Belief in God Properly Basic?" *Nous* (March 1981).

2. W. K. Clifford, "The Ethics of Belief," in *Lectures and Essays* (London: Macmillan, 1879).

3. Plantinga has now addressed himself to this difficulty in "The Reformed Objection to Natural Theology," in *Christian Scholar's Review* (1982), 11:3.

4. "On Believing Someone," in Delaney, ed., *Rationality and Religious Belief.*

Index

Index